Bread Mach[illegible] Reci[illegible]

A Quick and Easy Guide to Discovery New Recipes, to Bake Homemade Bread with Your Bread Machine

By

Michelle Crocker

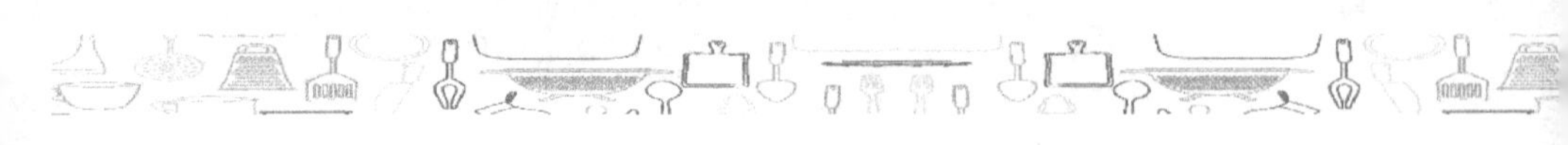

The information provided herein is stated to be truthful and consistent, in that any liability, in terms of inattention or otherwise, by any usage or abuse of any policies, processes, or Instructions contained within is the solitary and utter responsibility of the recipient reader. Under no circumstances will any legal responsibility or blame be held against the publisher for any reparation, damages, or monetary loss due to the information herein, either directly or indirectly. Respective authors own all copyrights not held by the publisher.

The information herein is offered for informational purposes solely and is universal as so. The presentation of the information is without contract or any type of guarantee assurance.

The trademarks that are used are without any consent and the publication of the trademark is without permission or backing by the trademark owner. All trademarks and brands within this book are for clarifying purposes only and are the owned by the owners themselves s, not affiliated with this document.

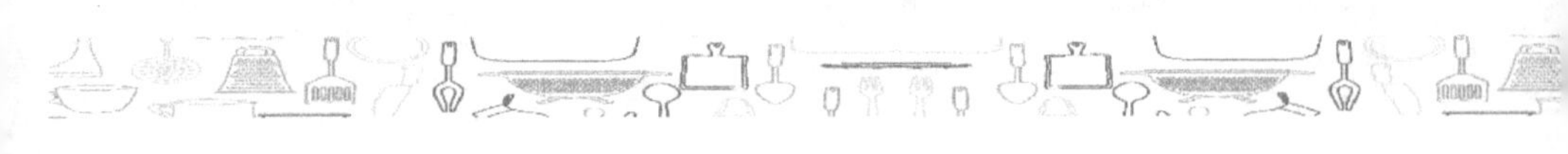

Introduction

Homemade bread is nutritious and tasty, but to make it from scratch requires a huge amount of work. It requires a lot of effort, time, and patience to combine the ingredients, knead the dough, wait for it to rise, knead it again, and then bake it, but it does not have to be always this way. The bread maker can do all the hard work, and you have only to taste and appreciate the wonderful taste of homemade bread. If one is not yet persuaded and wonders if it is wise to invest in such an appliance, all the recipes in this book can reassure you of its merit. The bread-making process is slow and labor-intensive, and as many people do not have the patience to go through the entire process in this time, bread machines have become a requirement.

Although a person can still buy bread from markets, it would always be a better choice to bake bread at home, as bread can be optimized as per the tastes and health needs of the individual/family. A home machine for baking bread is a bread machine that transforms all the ingredients into tasty bread. The wonderful thing about an automated bread maker is that all these steps are completed for you. Basically, a bread-making appliance is a portable electric oven that contains a single wide bread tin. The tin is still a little unique; it has a bottom axle that attaches to the electric motor below it. Within the tin, a small metal paddle spins on the axle. A waterproof seal holds the axle, so the bread mixture cannot leak. Bread has always been eaten along with all sorts of food, rendering it mandatory for all occasions, whether it be lunch, brunch, or dinner. Using a bread maker is better than purchasing the bread at a store.

Tore-bought bread is full of synthetic chemicals, but you only need natural ingredients at home with a bread

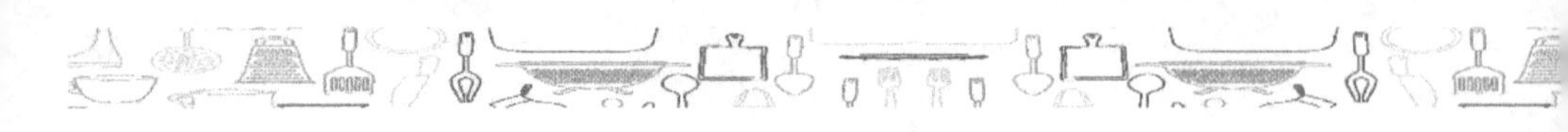

machine. You may even incorporate specific ingredients, including grains or seeds, to make it much better; apart from flour, you will need yeast and water. Homemade bread is even tastier given the fact that you must always use fresh ingredients, and you can personalize ingredients according to the particular preference. Even if that's not enough, after traditional bread-making, many dishes have to be washed too. One has to put in the ingredients with a bread machine, and after the bread is baked, clean the tin.

Current bread machines bring a lot of special controls that allow several bread specialties to be prepared. For individuals who are intolerant or sensitive to such foods, such as gluten, a bread machine may be especially useful. This book will provide you with all sorts of recipes. These devices can also be used for recipes other than bread, such as jelly, fruit jam, scrambled eggs, tomato sauce, and casseroles, and even some desserts, with a couple of ingredients variations. All you have to do is use fresh ingredients and walk away.

Chapter 1: Easy Baking with Bread Machine

Since the beginning of baking, freshly made bread is the best thing ever. The only trouble is, time and commitment are required. Many individuals have never baked bread in their lives and will never think of doing so, but much of that has begun to shift with the new advent of automated bread-making machines. Today millions convert their homes into bakeries, and every day one can enjoy their own freshly made bread at a fraction of the price they might spend in a shop. There are different explanations for why an individual should suggest using a bread maker instead of any other choices that he has access to.

Bread machines in cafes, households, workplaces, etc., have often been more comfortable people's choice. The majority of available bread makers on the market are automatic.

Bread machines reduce effort and time by helping their customers. An ingredient may be added to it by a baker, homemaker, or any

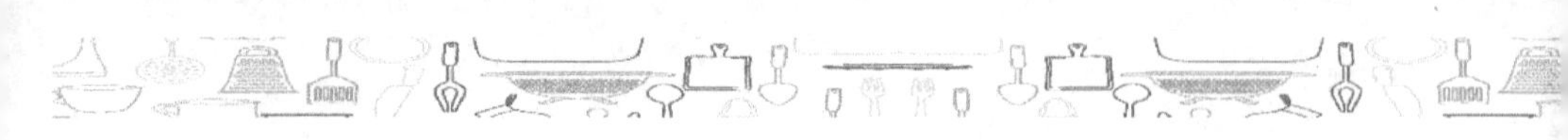

other user. It completes its work automatically, without any control on the part of its consumer. Bread machines allow consumers to do other required things, such as preparing the main course, dinner, etc., while reducing the workload.

It is necessary to remember, though, that not all bread machines are automated. Many Pricey bread makers only give automatic functions. To finish the bread-making method, you just need all the necessary ingredients. Bread makers are often simple to use and manage, much like ovens for bread makers. Assume an individual doesn't know how to bake or doesn't even want to bake; bread machines are the ideal substitute for those people. In addition, it is often likely that individuals wish to bake a certain form of bread at home, like French bread, but does not know how to use an oven for baking one. A bread maker allows us to produce such bread in these situations, while alternate cycles or settings also come with it.

The dough must go through 5 phases if you make bread the conventional way, primarily as mixing, kneading, rising, punching down, proving, and baking, but it's all in one move with the bread maker. All ingredients you have to add to the system, adjust the cycles, and let it do its thing. Each time, you'll get accurate outcomes.

1.1 Main Ingredients for Baking

Baking powder, produced from starch and tartar cream, is a fermenting agent that allows the batter to grow. It has an acidic ingredient incorporated into it, so one does not need to integrate something else for raising the flour. A bitter-tasting food can result from too much baking powder, whereas too little results in a hard cake with very little volume.

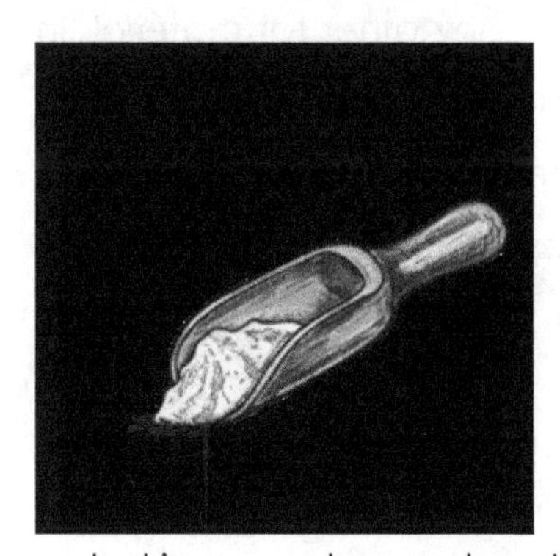

Baking soda is a simple sodium bicarbonate which has to be mixed with yogurt, honey, or cocoa, as an acidic ingredient. It's a fermenting product much like baking soda. Using baking soda too much will make the cake rough in texture. Baking soda and baking powder can lose their strength more easily than you would know. If the packages are not fresh, inspect them before using them. Place a couple of teaspoons of white vinegar in a tiny bowl to test the baking soda and incorporate a teaspoon of baking soda. It can vigorously foam out, and it will take some moments for the frothing to subside. The more bubbles, the stronger the baking soda would be. You should substitute the baking soda for fresh baking soda if there is no action, or it just ends up with a couple of tiny bubbles. To check the baking powder, add a spoon full of baking powder into a cup.

Fill the bowl with hot water to cover the baking powder; if it continues to burst furiously, it's safe to include it in the recipes. When weighing, do not add a wet spoon into the baking powder bag for better results.

The water can trigger the baking powder left unused in the can, and each time, it will not be as pleasant to use. If you can see lumps in the baking soda, it's typically a warning that humidity has made its way in the baking soda.

Butter, as a stable fat, butter is ideally used for baking than any other fat material. In fact, butter adds taste, with a melting point only below body temp. Hence certain cookies and bakery items appear to "melt in the

mouth."

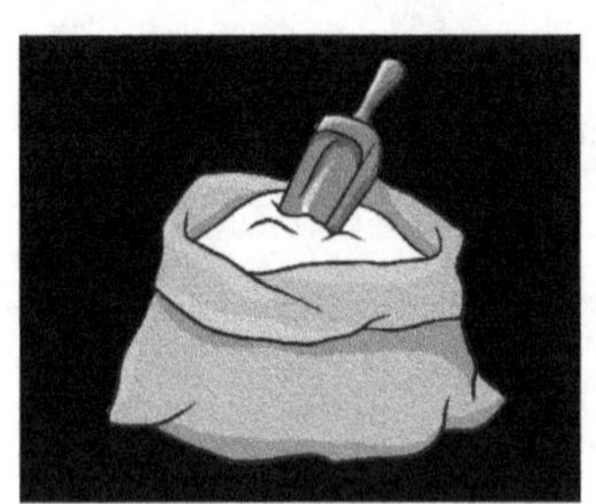

Cornstarch has many uses based on the kind of recipe it's being incorporated in. Cornstarch is commonly either a binder or thickener, although it may be an anti-caking agent as well.

It's perfect to use to thicken custards sauces or in gluten-free cooking.

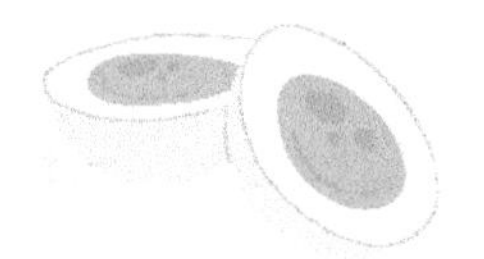

Eggs have many uses, but most significantly, they add volume to foods and are a binding agent, ensuring they hold together the final product.

For glazing, flavor, thickening, and binding, you can use the entire egg or just use the egg yolks and egg whites for different reasons. Egg whites, providing moisture and strength. Egg yolks contribute to shape and flavor.

Flour has a very crucial part in making bread. Its major quality is that it binds all the products together.

It transforms into gluten as flour protein is mixed with heat and moisture.

Different flour varieties have different protein amounts and are ideal for various bakery products.

Milk provides softness, moisture, taste, and lightens color to baked goods.

It provides a double function since it adds structure and strength to the batter or dough and provides tenderness, flavor, and moisture.

Sugar, in every particular recipe, sugar is executing a variety of functions. It provides texture, moisture, and holds the form.

Although operating in combination with eggs, fat, and liquid materials, it is also just another rising agent. Sugar gives "crunch" to certain cookies and cakes.

1.2 Bread Machine Cycles

Like in any other bread making, the bread machine also goes through cycles to make you the flavorful bread.

1.2.1 Kneading Cycle

The first cycle is kneading, and perhaps the most significant step in baking bread that includes yeast. Kneading combines all the ingredients absolutely well and is probably the bread machine's noisiest period. It will also take anywhere between 15 to 45minutes for this cycle. The time it takes depends on the bread machine, and the sort of bread one is making. In most machines at the bottom of the baking tin, kneading propellers completely combine everything.

1.2.2 Rest Cycle

The rest cycle makes the dough rest until it begins kneading again. Autolyzing is the scientific baking word for this. Essentially, it helps the moisture surrounding the dough to soak in the starch and gluten completely. It can take this process from only a couple of minutes to over 35 minutes.

1.2.3 Rise Cycle

It would require this cycle if the flour has gluten in it, so it will rise and make the bread airy and soft. It is a fermentation. Depending on the bread machine, this cycle can normally take about 40 to 50 minutes. It can take considerably longer occasionally, particularly if you're making French bread.

1.2.4 Punch Cycle

The next cycle is Punch Cycle after the dough has finished the rising cycle. In this cycle, the bread machine continues to knead the dough yet again. The distinction is that it is performed even more lightly at this point, and the goal is to remove the small air pockets

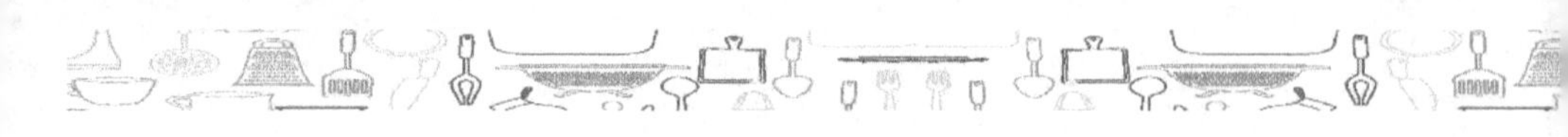

produced in the growing period by the fermentation of the yeast. Usually, the Punch cycle, often referred to as the shape-forming cycle, is a short cycle that takes only seconds to complete, and it is still necessary.

1.2.5 Baking Cycle

This is the most important cycle. This is the cycle in which the bread maker bakes the bread. Depending on the bread maker and the kind of bread you are making, this cycle will take anywhere from half an hour to more than 90 minutes.

Other important baking modes of the bread machine are

- Basic Bread
- Sweet Bread
- Whole-Wheat Cycle
- Gluten-Free Bread
- Rapid Bake
- Cake & Jam—yes, you can make Jellies and Jam and sauces.

1.3 How easy are Bread Machines to use?

Bread machines are very easy and simple to use. Add in ingredients specifically in an order, following the bread machine's manufacturer suggested order. In most machines, add liquids first, then in dry ingredients, or as your machine specifies. All ingredients should be at room temperature or specified otherwise.

- Choose the type of bread you want to make (whole wheat, sweet, basic, multigrain, pizza, or French).
- Choose the baking mode (bake rapid, bake, sandwich, or dough). Choosing different modes changes the sequence of kneading, mixing, rising, and baking. In dough mode, for example, the bread maker will stop without actually baking the bread. You can open up the lid, take out the dough, and roll it out however you like. After that, you have to bake in the oven rather than a bread machine.
- Choose the bread loaf size if your machine has this feature. (1 lb., 1.5 lb. or 2 lb.).
- Choose the crust type to your liking.
- Click the Timer button if your machine has one. The bread maker will show you the time it will take to bake the bread.
- Now click the Start button, and your wait begins.
- When the loaf is baked (from three to four hours), you slowly open the lid, take the heated tin out of the bread machine, wait for ten or more minutes to take out the loaf, let it cool

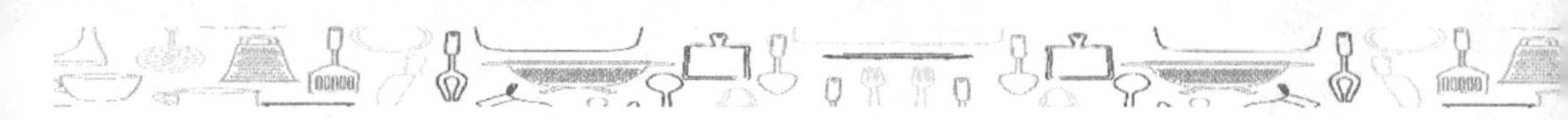

off. In the cleaning process, you only have to wipe out the tin (which is non-stick), requiring only 30 seconds.

1.4 Choosing the Right Bread Machine

Think of yourself what the criteria will be before selecting the right kind of bread machine for yourself.

Timer: You can manually determine when to set the timer for a baking cycle. Then you have to come at the right time, to take the bread out of the maker. Otherwise, the bread would be preheated and cooked, or choose a one where the machine will calculate the time.

Size: Get the bread machine that carries a recipe comprising 3 cups of flour if one has a big family. Some can hold flour cups of up to 4 to 5-1/2.

Blades: Blades in horizontal pans do not often knead the dough too well, leaving the pan's corners with flour. A big negative is incomplete blending. However, the upright settings do a better job of mixing. Many new machines are made vertically, but some horizontal pans also offer two blades, so choose carefully.

How expensive does a bread machine be?

Some automated control machines are a bit pricey since they do not need your supervision, but some machines require your full-time attention, so keep that fact in mind.

1.5 Mistakes to Avoid While Using the Bread Maker

Here are some tips that will help you to avoid making mistakes while using a bread machine

- You must unplug the appliance before taking bread out.
- Failing to measure the ingredients precisely
- You must add ingredients accepted by the bread machine in the order suggested.
- Please consider the Kitchen's temperature.
- Not opening the lid: it's a good idea to open the lid and look at the dough, particularly in the kneading process, for about after ten minutes. Look at the dough's surface if it's too sticky and requires more flour if your finger is covered in the dough.

  If the dough looks too dry, so it needs more water. Adding products is better than taking them out, so incorporate a vigilant quantity at once. To re-adjust the texture, add a teaspoon of water or flour at a time.
- As the bread bakes, you leave paddles in the machine: You can hear the bread maker begin beating down the dough before the bread reaches the final rise process. Now open the lid, shift the flour to the side of the tin, and gently bring the paddles out.

- Enabling the loaf to rise without reshaping the dough in the final period.
- Taking the bread out before it cools, try waiting for ten to fifteen minutes before taking out the bread.

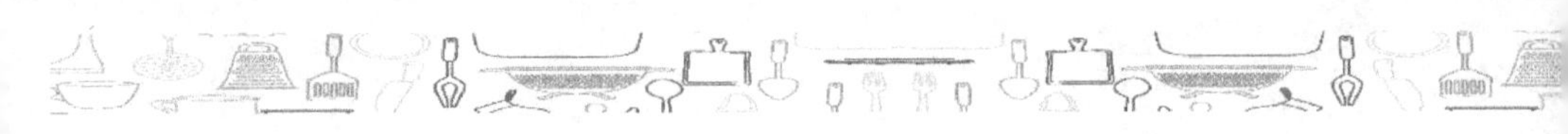

1.6 Benefits of Using Bread Machine

- It is easier to bake bread in a bread machine.
- The process is cleaner and simpler than traditional bread baking.
- Every time the bread machine produces the same consistency & exceptional taste.
- The benefit of jam and jelly making.
- You're not going to do the kneading.
- Make your fresh bread, at home, for the sandwiches.
- You can add many ingredients to make the bread to your taste.
- It is convenient for busy people.
- Saves long-term resources and money.

Chapter 2: Basic Breads

2.1 English Muffin Bread

(Prep time: 15 minutes | Total time: 3 hours 40 minutes)

Ingredients

- Lukewarm milk: 1 cup
- Vinegar: 1 teaspoon
- Butter: 2 tablespoons
- 1/3 to 1/4 cup of water
- 1 and a half teaspoons of salt
- Instant yeast: 2 and 1/4 teaspoons
- 3 and a half cups of all-purpose flour
- 1 and a half teaspoons of sugar
- Half teaspoon of baking powder

Instructions

- In the tin of bread machine, add all ingredients. Use less water in a humid environment and more water in a dry or colder environment.
- Select basic and light crust. Press start. Adjust dough consistency by adding more flour if too sticky and add water if too dry.

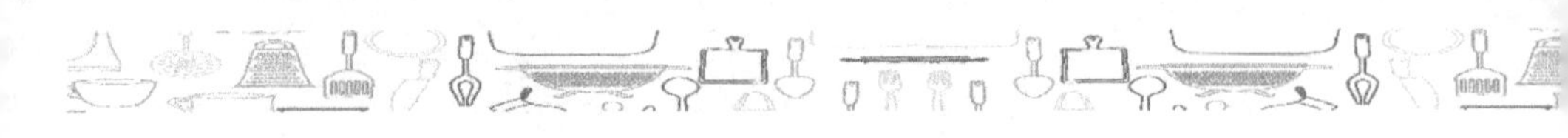

- Serve fresh.

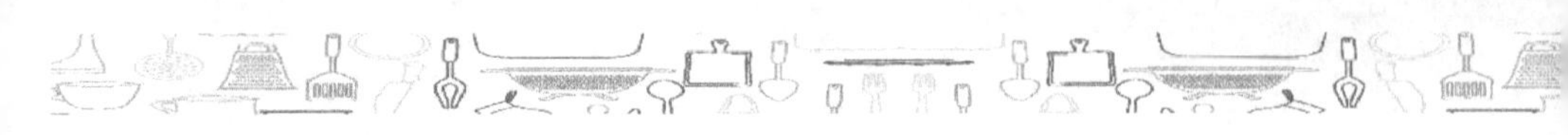

2.2 Cocoa Bread

(Prep time: 10 minutes | Total time: 3 hours 5 minutes)

Ingredients

- 1 whole egg
- 1 cup of milk
- One yolk only
- Salt: 1 teaspoon
- Canola oil: 3 tablespoons
- Vanilla extract: 1 teaspoon
- Wheat gluten: 1 tablespoon
- 3 cups of bread flour
- Half cup of brown sugar
- 2 and a half teaspoons of bread machine yeast
- Cocoa powder: 1/3 cup

Instructions

- Add all the ingredients in the bread machine in the suggested order by the manufacturer.
- Select white bread, medium crust. Press start.
- Serve fresh.

2.3 Anise Lemon Bread

(Prep time: 10 minutes | Total time: 3 hours 5 minutes)

Ingredients

- Water
- 1 lemon: juice and zest
- Olive oil: 1 tablespoon
- Half cup of milk (110 F).
- 2 tablespoons of honey
- Instant active dry yeast: 3 teaspoons
- Anise seeds: 1 tablespoon
- 1 teaspoon of salt
- 3 cups of bread flour

Instructions

- Add lemon juice to a cup and enough lukewarm water to make a half cup.
- Heat this mixture to 110 F.
- Add to the bread machine, then lemon zest and rest of the ingredients.
- Select basic and crust to your liking—press start.

- After 10 minutes, check the dough's consistency. Add more flour or water if required.
- Serve fresh.

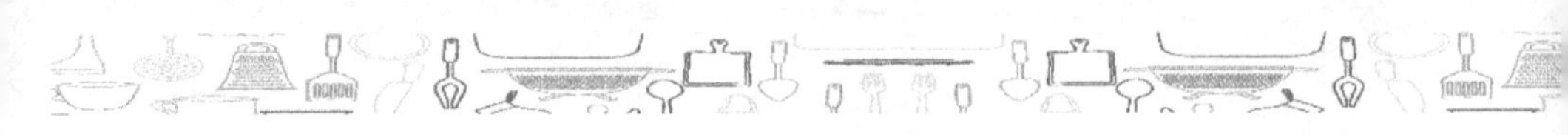

2.4 Fragrant Cardamom Bread

(Prep time: 5 minutes | Total time: 1 hour 5 minutes)

Ingredients

- 1 whole egg
- Half cup of milk
- Honey: 1/4 cup
- Ground cardamom: 1 teaspoon
- Unsweetened applesauce: 1/4 cup
- Active dry yeast: 2 teaspoons
- 1 teaspoon of salt
- Bread flour: 2 and a 3/4 cups

Instructions

- Add all ingredients to the bread machine in the suggested order by the manufacturer.
- Select basic, light crust—press start.
- Serve warm with butter.

2.5 Chocolate Mint Bread

(Prep time: 10 minutes | Total time: 3 hours 5 minutes)

Ingredients

- Softened butter: 2 tablespoons
- Water: 1 and a 1/4 cups + 2 tbsp.
- 1 and a 1/4 teaspoons of salt
- 4 cups of bread flour
- 2 and a half teaspoons of bread machine dry yeast
- Sugar: 1/3 cup
- Mint chocolate chips: 2/3 cup

Instructions

- Carefully measure and place all ingredients in the bread pan as per the order suggested by the manufacturer.
- Select the sweet cycle. Light crust. Press start.
- Serve fresh.

2.6 Molasses Candied-Ginger Bread

(Prep time: 10 minutes | Total time: 3 hours 10 minutes)

Ingredients

- Molasses: 1⁄4 cup
- 3 and 1⁄3 cups of bread flour
- 1 whole egg
- Milk: 3⁄4 cup
- 3 tablespoons of butter
- Brown sugar: 1 tablespoon
- Ginger: 3⁄4 teaspoon
- Raisins: 1⁄3 cup
- Salt: 3⁄4 teaspoon
- Cinnamon: 3⁄4 teaspoon
- Active dry yeast: 2 and a 1⁄4 teaspoons

Instructions

- Add all ingredients to the bread machine in the suggested order by the manufacturer. Do not add raisins yet.
- Select white bread and light crust—press start.
- Add raisins on ingredient beeping.
- Serve warm.

2.7 Dark Rye Bread

(Prep time: 5 minutes | Total time: 3 hours 10 minutes)

Ingredients

- 2 and a half cups of bread flour
- Warm water: 1 and 1⁄4 cups
- Yeast: 2 and 1⁄4 teaspoons
- 1 cup of rye flour
- Molasses: 1⁄3 cup
- Half teaspoon of salt
- Caraway seed: 1 tablespoon
- Vegetable oil: 1⁄8 cup
- Cocoa powder: 1⁄8 cup

Instructions

- Add ingredients in the bread machine in the suggested order by the manufacturer.
- Select white bread—press start.
- Serve fresh

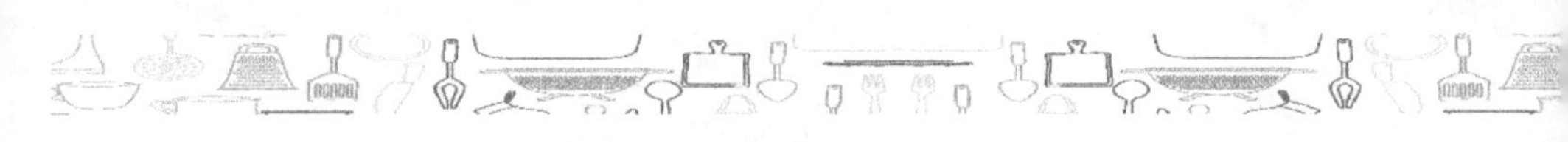

2.8 Golden Raisin Bread

(Prep time: 10 minutes | Total time: 3 hours 10 minutes)

Ingredients

- 1 Cup of quick Oatmeal
- Warm Milk: 1 and 1/3 Cups
- 2 Teaspoons of Bread Machine Yeast
- 3 Cups of Bread Flour
- Half cup of Brown Sugar
- Molasses: 2 Teaspoons
- Sliced Butter: 4 Tablespoons
- Golden Raisins: 1 Cup
- Salt: 2 Teaspoons

Instructions

- Add all ingredients except raisins to the bread machine in the suggested order by the manufacturer.
- Select basic, light crust and 2 lb. loaf.
- Press start.
- After the machine completes its first cycle of kneading, add raisins.
- Serve fresh.

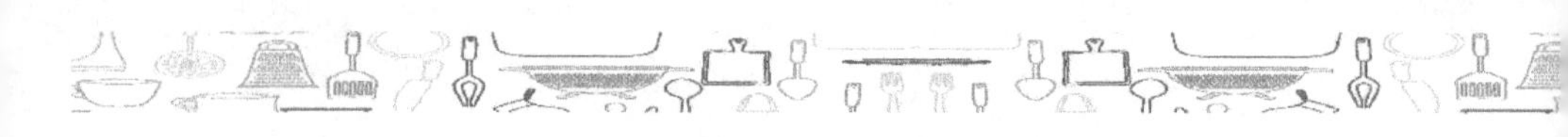

Chapter 3: Grain, Seed & Nuts Breads

3.1 Sunflower Bread

(Prep time: 10 minutes | Total time: 2 hours 10 minutes)

Ingredients

- 2 and a half cups of white bread flour
- 1 and 1⁄4 cups of water
- Dry milk: 2 tablespoons
- Half cup of sunflower seeds
- Half teaspoon of salt
- Wheat bread flour: 3⁄4 cup
- Butter: 2 tablespoons
- Fast rise yeast: 2 teaspoons
- Honey: 3 tablespoons

Instructions

- Add all ingredients to the bread machine in the suggested order by the manufacturer.
- Select the cycle you like the best. Even use the delay cycle.

- Press start and enjoy fresh bread.

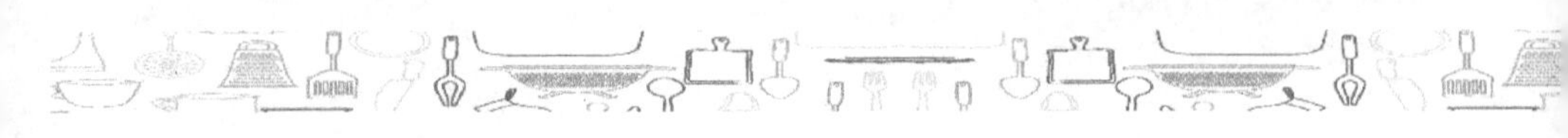

3.2 Raisin Seed Bread

(Prep time: 10 minutes | Total time: 3 hours 10 minutes)

Ingredients

- Cinnamon: 2 teaspoons
- Half teaspoon of salt
- Whole-wheat flour: 3 cups
- 1 cup of warm water
- Raisins: 1 cup
- Four tablespoons of honey
- One teaspoon of seeds
- Half cup of coconut oil
- Active dry yeast: 2 teaspoons

Instructions

- Add all ingredients to the bread machine in the suggested order by the manufacturer.
- Select whole-wheat crust to your liking—press start.

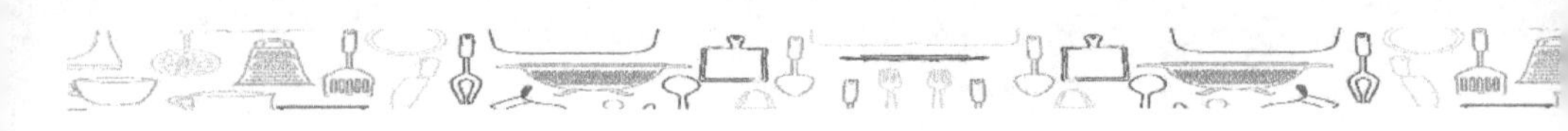

3.3 Quinoa Oatmeal Bread

(Prep time: 10 minutes | Total time: 3 hours 50 minutes)

Ingredients

- Half cup of whole wheat flour
- Buttermilk: 1 cup
- 1 and a half of bread flour
- Half cup of quick-cooking oats
- 1 and a half teaspoons of bread machine yeast
- 2/3 cup of water
- Honey: 1 tablespoon
- 1/3 cup of uncooked quinoa
- 4 tablespoons of melted unsalted butter
- Salt: 1 teaspoon
- Sugar: 1 tablespoon

Instructions

- Cook quinoa in 2/3 cup of water. Cool it.
- Add all ingredients with cooked quinoa to the bread machine in the suggested order by the manufacturer.
- Select whole grain and press start.
- Enjoy fresh.

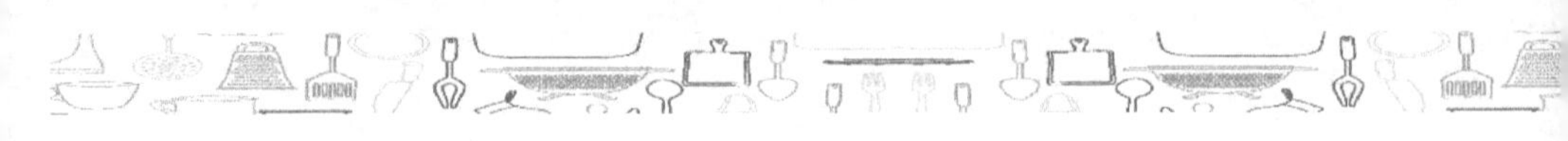

3.4 Rich Cheddar Bread

(Prep time: 10 minutes | Total time: 3 hours 10 minutes)

Ingredients

- 2 and a half tablespoons of Parmesan cheese
- 1 cup of warm water
- Half teaspoon of salt
- 3 and a half teaspoons of sugar
- 1 and a 1/4 cup of freshly grated cheddar cheese
- Dry mustard: 1 teaspoon
- 2 and a half tablespoons of softened butter
- 2 and a half cups of bread flour
- 1 and a half teaspoons of paprika
- Active dry yeast: 2 teaspoons
- 2 and a half tablespoons of minced onions

Instructions

- Place all ingredients in the bread machine in the suggested order by the manufacturer.
- Select white setting, crust to your liking.

- Press start and assess dough's consistency if it needs water or more flour.
- Add one tbsp. of flour or water if required.
- Serve fresh.

3.5 Feta Oregano Bread

(Prep time: 10 minutes | Total time: 3 hours 10 minutes)

Ingredients

- 1 and a half tablespoons of olive oil
- 3 cups of bread flour
- Half cup of crumbled feta cheese
- 1 cup of water
- Active dry yeast: 2 teaspoons
- Dried leaf oregano: 1 tablespoon
- Salt: 1 teaspoon
- 3 tablespoons of sugar

Instructions

- Put all ingredients in the bread machine in the suggested order by the manufacturer.
- Select basic. Press start.
- Serve fresh.

3.6 Mozzarella-Herb Bread

(Prep time: 10 minutes | Total time: 3 hours 10 minutes)

Ingredients

- Onion Powder: 1 Teaspoon
- Butter cut into slices: 6 Tablespoons
- lukewarm Milk: 1/3 Cup
- Bread Flour: 4 Cups
- 1 and a half teaspoons of Bread Machine Yeast
- 2 Tablespoons of Sugar
- Italian Herb Seasoning: 2 Tablespoons
- 1 and a half Teaspoons of Salt

Instructions

- Add all ingredients to the bread machine in the suggested order by the manufacturer.
- Select basic, light crust—press start.
- Before the baking cycle begins, sprinkle Italian seasoning on top.
- Enjoy fresh.

3.7 Simple Garlic Bread

(Prep time: 10 minutes | Total time: 3 hours 15 minutes)

Ingredients

- 1 tablespoon of butter
- Warm water: 1 cup (110 F)
- Powdered milk: 1 tablespoon
- White sugar: 1 tablespoon
- 1 and a half teaspoons of salt
- Active dry yeast: 2 teaspoons
- Minced garlic: 3 teaspoons
- 1 and a half tablespoons of dried parsley
- Bread flour: 3 cups

Instructions

- Add all ingredients to the bread machine in the suggested order by the manufacturer.
- Select the basic cycle, and press start.
- Serve fresh.

3.8 Herbed Pesto Bread

(Prep time: 10 minutes | Total time: 2 hours 5 minutes)

Ingredients

- 3 cups bread flour
- 1 and a half teaspoons of sugar
- 1 cup of water
- 1 teaspoon salt
- Pesto sauce: 1/4 cup
- 2 and a 1/4 teaspoons of bread machine yeast
- Lemon juice: 1 teaspoon

Instructions

- Add all ingredients to the bread machine in the suggested order by the manufacturer.
- Select basic cycle and 1.5 lb.
- Press start and serve fresh.

Chapter 4: Fruit Breads

4.1 Fragrant Orange Bread

(Prep time: 10 minutes | Total time: 3 hours 45 minutes)

Ingredients

- Half teaspoon of grated orange
- orange juice concentrate: 3 tablespoons
- 1 whole egg
- 3 cups of bread flour
- 1 and a ¼ teaspoons of salt
- Water: half cup+1 tablespoon
- Granulated sugar: ¼ cup
- Instant dry milk: 2 tablespoons
- 1 and a half tablespoons of softened butter
- Bread machine yeast: 2 teaspoons

For Orange Glaze

- Orange juice: 1 tablespoon
- ¾ cup of powdered sugar

Instructions

- Add all ingredients to the bread machine in the suggested order by the manufacturer.
- Select the white cycle. Do not use the delay feature. Select Light crust—press start.
- Meanwhile, mix the glaze ingredients.

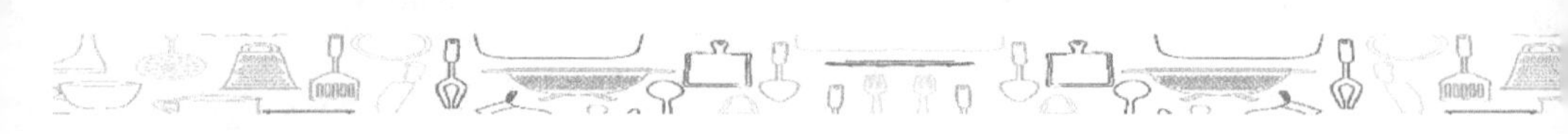

- Drizzle the glaze over fresh bread.

4.2 Moist Oatmeal Apple Bread

(Prep time: 10 minutes | Total time: 3 hours 10 minutes)

Ingredients

- Unsweetened applesauce: 1/3 cup
- Water: 1/3 cup
- Unsweetened apple juice: 2/3 cup
- 3 tablespoons of honey
- Oat bran: 1/4 cup
- 2 tablespoons of vegetable oil
- Quick-cooking oats: 1/3 cup
- 1 and a half teaspoons of salt
- Bread flour: 3 cups
- 2 and a 1/4 teaspoons of bread machine yeast
- 1 and a half teaspoons of ground cinnamon

Instructions

- Add all ingredients to the bread machine in the suggested order by the manufacturer.
- Select basic cycle, light crust. Press start.
- Serve fresh bread.

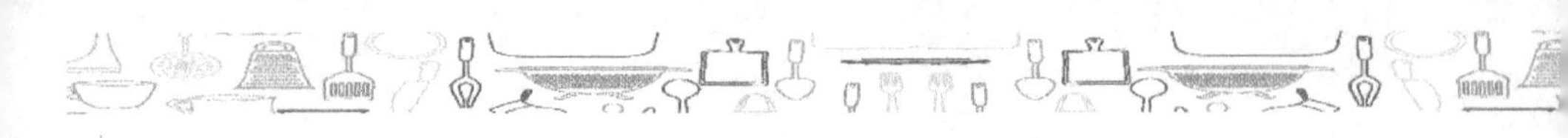

4.3 Strawberry Shortcake Bread

(Prep time: 10 minutes | Total time: 3 hours 10 minutes)

Ingredients

- 2 and a half teaspoons of bread machine yeast
- Vanilla extract: 1 teaspoon
- Warm heavy whipping cream: 1/4 cup
- Bread machine flour: 3 cups
- 1/4 cup of warm water
- Sugar: 1 tablespoon
- Baking powder: 1/8 teaspoon
- 2 cups of fresh strawberries with 1/4 cup sugar
- Salt: 1 teaspoon

Instructions

- Add water, cream to the pan of the bread maker, mix with yeast and sugar. Let it rest for 15 minutes.
- Coat the sliced strawberries with ¼ cup of sugar.
- Add all ingredients, except for strawberries, to the bread machine in the manufacturer's suggested order.
- Add strawberries to the fruit hopper or add at the ingredients signal.
- Select basic, medium crust. Press start.

- Slice and serve fresh bread.

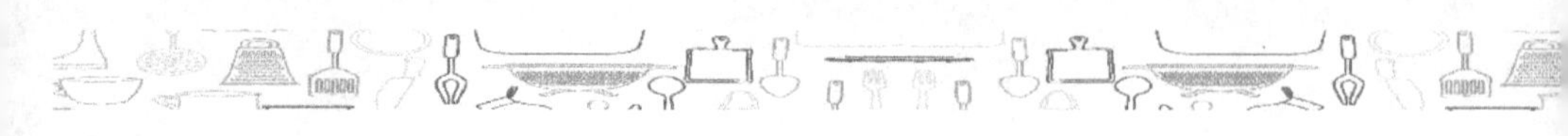

4.4 Golden Butternut Squash Raisin Bread

(Prep time: 10 minutes | Total time: 3 hours 10 minutes)

Ingredients

- Bread flour: 3 cups
- Nonfat milk powder: 3 tbsp.
- Active dry yeast: 4 tsp.
- Wheat germ: 3 tbsp.
- Gluten four: 3 tbsp.
- Salt: one and a half tsp.
- Butter: 3 tbsp.
- Butternut puree: 1 cup
- Water: 2/3 cup
- Raisins: half cup
- Sugar: 4 tbsp.
- Ground ginger: half tsp.
- Ground cinnamon: ¾ tsp

Instructions

- Add all ingredients to the bread machine in the suggested order by the manufacturer.

- Select basic and crust to your liking—press start.
- Serve fresh bread.

4.5 Sweet Potato Bread

(Prep time: 10 minutes | Total time: 3 hours 10 minutes)

Ingredients

- Half teaspoon of cinnamon
- Half cup of Luke warm water
- Flour: 4 cups
- Vanilla extract: 1 teaspoon
- 1/3 cup of packed brown sugar
- Butter: 2 tablespoons, softened
- 1 and a half teaspoons of salt
- Mashed sweet potatoes: 1 cup
- 2 tablespoons of powdered milk
- Yeast: 2 teaspoons

Instructions

- Add all ingredients to the bread machine in the suggested order by the manufacturer.
- Select white bread, light crust. Press start.
- Serve fresh bread.'

4.6 Potato Thyme Bread

(Prep time: 10 minutes | Total time: 3 hours 10 minutes)

Ingredients

- 1 and a half tsp of salt
- 2 tbsp. of butter softened
- 1 tbsp. of sugar
- 1.25 cups of lukewarm (110 F) water
- Bread machine yeast: 2 tsp
- Instant potato flakes: half cup
- Bread flour: 3 cups
- Dried thyme leaves: 2 tbsp.

Instructions

- Add all ingredients to the bread machine in the suggested order by the manufacturer.
- Select white cycle and dark crust if you like.
- Press start.
- Serve fresh bread.

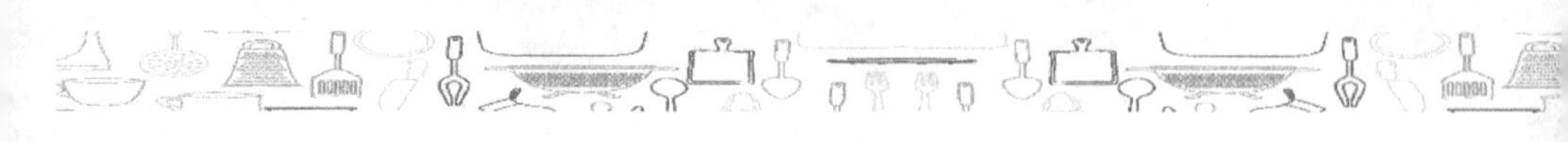

4.7 Light Corn Bread

(Prep time: 10 minutes | Total time: 3 hours 10 minutes)

Ingredients

- 1 cup of milk
- 1/4 cup of sugar
- 2 whole eggs – lightly whisked
- 1 and a 1/4 cup of bread flour
- Baking powder: 4 teaspoons
- 1 cup of cornmeal
- 1/4 cup of melted butter
- Salt: 1 teaspoon
- Vanilla: 1 teaspoon

Instructions

- Add all ingredients to the bread machine in the suggested order by the manufacturer.
- Use cake cycle/quick cycle and a light crust. Press start.
- Serve fresh bread

4.8 Hot Red Pepper Bread

(Prep time: 10 minutes | Total time: 3 hours 10 minutes)

Ingredients

- Butter: 1 tablespoon
- Unsweetened yogurt: 2 tablespoons
- 2 cloves of garlic
- 3 cups of bread flour
- 3 tablespoons of parmesan cheese
- Roasted red pepper: 1⁄4 cup, chopped
- 1 and a half teaspoons of dried basil
- Water: 3⁄4 cup
- 2 tablespoons of sugar
- 2 teaspoons bread machine yeast
- 1 and a half teaspoons of salt

Instructions

- Add all ingredients to the bread machine in the suggested order by the manufacturer.
- Set basic setting, Light crust. Press start.Serve fresh bread.

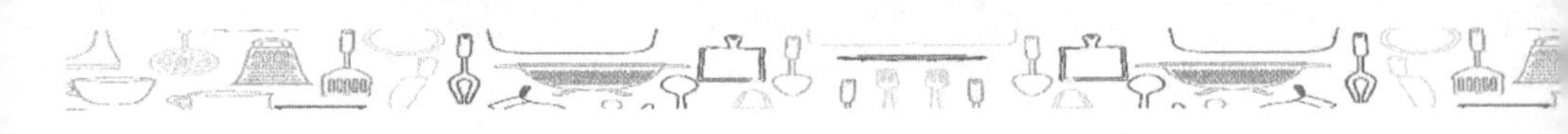

Chapter 5: Sourdough Breads

5.1 Herb Sourdough

(Prep time: 10 minutes | Total time: 3 hours 10 minutes)

Ingredients

- 3 tablespoons of sugar
- 3⁄4 cup of water
- 1 and a half teaspoons of salt
- 3 or 3 and a half cups of bread flour
- dried parsley: 1 teaspoon
- 1 1⁄4 cups of sourdough starter
- 1 and a half teaspoons of dried Rosemary
- Soy margarine: 2 tablespoons

Instructions

- Add all ingredients to the bread machine in the suggested order by the manufacturer.
- Start with three cups of flour. Select basic cycle, light crust. Press start.

- Check dough after 5-10 minutes; if it needs more flour, then add one tbsp. of flour at a time.
- Serve fresh bread.

5.2 Cranberry Pecan Sourdough

(Prep time: 10 minutes | Total time: 3 hours 10 minutes)

Ingredients

- 1 dried package of (3 and a half ounce) sweetened cranberries
- Water: 2 tablespoons + 1 and a ¼ cup
- Salt: 2 teaspoons
- Chopped pecans: 3⁄4 cup, toasted
- Bread flour: 4 cups
- Butter: 2 tablespoons
- 2 teaspoons of yeast
- Non-fat powdered milk: 2 tablespoons
- 1⁄4 cup of sugar

Instructions

- Place all ingredients in the bread machine as per the suggested order by the manufacturer.
- Select white bread setting, medium crust. Press start.
- Enjoy fresh bread.

5.3 Dark Chocolate Sourdough

(Prep time: 10 minutes | Total time: 3 hours 10 minutes)

Ingredients

- Lukewarm (110 F) Water: 3⁄4 cup
- Half cup of cocoa powder
- Sourdough starter: 1 cup
- Sugar: 1 tablespoon
- dark chocolate: Half cup, finely diced
- 3 tablespoons of oil
- 2 teaspoons of salt
- Active dry yeast: 1 tablespoon
- 3 cups of bread flour

Instructions

- Add all ingredients to the bread machine in the suggested order by the manufacturer.
- Select basic cycle. Light crust. Press start.
- Check dough's consistency if it's too wet and sticky and requires more flour. Add one tbsp. of flour at a time.
- Serve fresh bread.

5.4 Banana Coconut Bread

(Prep time: 10 minutes | Total time: 3 hours 10 minutes)

Ingredients

- 8 tablespoons of sugar
- 3 large ripe bananas
- 1 tsp. of baking powder
- 2 cups of plain flour
- 1 tsp. of salt
- Half cup of coconut flakes
- 2 whole eggs
- Half tsp. of vanilla
- Half tsp. of cinnamon

Instructions

- Mix the sugar with mashed bananas.
- Add all ingredients to the bread machine in the suggested order by the manufacturer.
- Select basic cycle. Press start.
- Enjoy fresh bread.

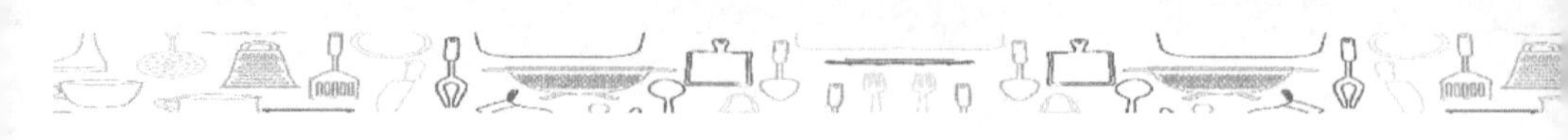

5.5 Easy Honey Beer Bread

(Prep time: 10 minutes | Total time: 1 hour 45 minutes)

Ingredients

- 2 tablespoons of olive oil
- 3⁄4 teaspoon of salt
- 3 and a half cups of bread flour
- 1 and a 3⁄4 teaspoons of fast-rising yeast
- 1 and 1⁄8 cups of flat beer
- 1⁄4 cup of honey

Instructions

- Add all ingredients to the bread machine in the suggested order by the manufacturer.
- Select basic cycle. Press start.
- Enjoy fresh bread.

5.6 Coffee Molasses Bread

(Prep time: 10 minutes | Total time: 2 hours 40 minutes)

Ingredients

- 3 tablespoons of honey
- Butter: 2 tablespoons
- 1 and a half teaspoons of salt
- 3 cups of bread flour
- 1 whole egg, whisked
- Instant coffer mixed in 1 cup of boiling water
- 1 tablespoon of dark molasses
- Half cup of oats
- 2 teaspoons of yeast

Instructions

- Mix oats with one cup of boiling water and set it aside. Let them come to

  110 F or lukewarm temperature.
- Add all ingredients to the bread machine in the suggested order by the manufacturer.
- Select basic cycle. Light crust. Press start.
- Serve fresh bread.

5.7 Pear Sweet Potato Bread

(Prep time: 10 minutes | Total time: 2 hours 25 minutes)

Ingredients

- Half teaspoon of almond extract
- 1 can of undrained (15 ounces) pear halves
- Mashed sweet potatoes: half cup
- 1 and a half teaspoons of salt
- 2 tablespoons of softened butter
- 3 and a half cups of bread flour
- 1 teaspoon of ground cinnamon
- 2 and a 1/4 teaspoons of active dry yeast
- 1/4 teaspoon of ground nutmeg

Instructions

- Puree the pear halves and juice in the blender. Add to the bread machine.
- Add the rest of the ingredients to the bread machine in the suggested order by the manufacturer.
- Select basic cycle. Press start.
- Enjoy fresh bread.

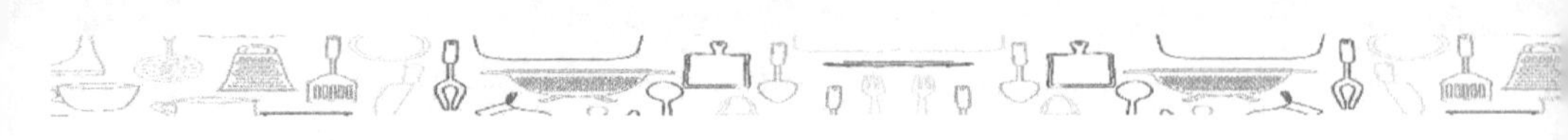

5.8 Sourdough Beer Bread

(Prep time: 10 minutes | Total time: 3 hours 10 minutes)

Ingredients

- Vegetable oil: 2 tablespoons
- 1 and 1⁄3 cups of sourdough starter
- Half cup of flat beer
- Bread flour: 3 cups
- 1 and a half teaspoons of salt
- 1⁄4 cup of water
- 1 and a half teaspoons of yeast
- Sugar: 1 tablespoon

Instructions

- Add all ingredients to the bread machine in the suggested order by the manufacturer.
- Select white bread, dark crust if you like—press start.
- Enjoy fresh bread.

Chapter 6: Holiday Breads

6.1 Julekake

(Prep time: 10 minutes | Total time: 3 hours 10 minutes)

Ingredients

- Bread machine yeast: 1 teaspoon
- Half teaspoon of ground cardamom
- 1 teaspoon of salt
- 1 egg mixed with enough water to make 1 cup and 2 tablespoons
- Sugar: 1 tbsp. + 1 tsp.
- Mixed candied fruit: 1/3 cup
- ¼ cup of softened butter
- Bread flour: 3 cups
- 1/3 cup of raisins

Instructions

- Add all ingredients, except candied fruits and raisins, to the bread machine in the manufacturer's suggested order.
- Select white bread cycle. Medium or light crust. Press start.
- Add candied fruit and raisins at the nut signal.

6.2 Spiked Eggnog Bread

(Prep time: 10 minutes | Total time: 3 hours 10 minutes)

Ingredients

- 3 cups of bread flour
- 1 and a 1⁄4 teaspoons of yeast
- 3⁄4 teaspoon of salt
- Half cup of eggnog
- 1⁄4 cup of milk
- 1 whole egg
- 2 tablespoons of sugar
- Half cup of glace cherries, cut into halves
- 2 tablespoons of butter, diced
- Half teaspoon of nutmeg

Instructions

- Place all ingredients in the bread machine, except cherries, in the suggested order by the manufacturer.
- Select basic cycle. Medium crust. Press start.
- Add cherries at the ingredient signal.
- Serve fresh bread.

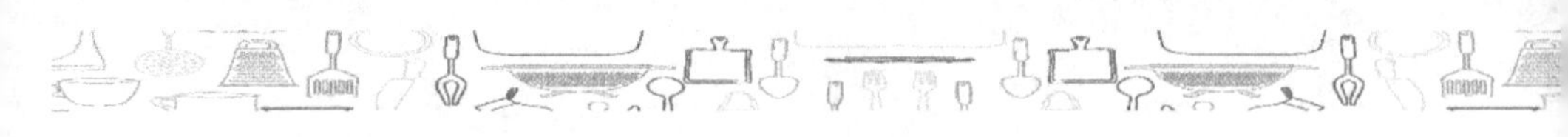

6.3 Hot Buttered Rum Bread

(Prep time: 10 minutes | Total time: 3 hours 40 minutes)

Instructions

- 1 tablespoon of rum extract
- 1 whole egg
- Softened Butter: 3 tablespoons
- 3 cups of bread flour
- 1 and a ¼ teaspoons of salt
- Half teaspoon of ground cinnamon
- Bread machine: 1 teaspoon
- ¼ teaspoon of ground nutmeg
- 3 tablespoons of brown sugar, packed
- ¼ teaspoon of ground cardamom

Nuts Topping

- 1 and a half teaspoons of packed brown sugar
- 1 and a half teaspoons of pecans, finely chopped
- 1 egg yolk, beaten

Instructions

- Mix the whole egg with water to make one cup. Place in the bread machine.

- Add the rest of the ingredients to the bread machine in the suggested order by the manufacturer.
- Select sweet cycle: light or medium crust. Do not use the delay feature.
- Press start.
- Meanwhile, mix all ingredients of topping in the bowl. Before the baking cycle begins, brush the topping on the loaf.
- Enjoy fresh bread.

6.4 Triple Chocolate Bread

(Prep time: 10 minutes | Total time: 3 hours 40 minutes)

Ingredients

- Vanilla extract: 1 tsp.
- Bread flour: 2 cups
- 2 tablespoons brown sugar
- 1 tablespoon margarine or butter
- Milk: 2/3 cup
- 1 teaspoon of active dry yeast
- 1 tablespoon unsweetened cocoa
- Half teaspoon of salt
- One whole egg
- Half cup of semisweet chocolate chips

Instructions

- Add all ingredients to the bread machine in the suggested order by the manufacturer.
- Select basic cycle. Press start.
- Enjoy fresh bread.

6.5 Chocolate Oatmeal Banana Bread

(Prep time: 10 minutes | Total time: 3 hours 40 minutes)

Ingredients

- 1 ounce of milk
- 2 bananas, mashed
- 1/3 cup of melted butter
- Bread flour: 2 cups
- 2 whole eggs
- Half tsp of salt
- Sugar: 2/3 cups
- Baking powder: 1.25 tsp

- Half cup of chocolate chips
- Half tsp of baking soda
- Half cup of chopped walnuts

Instructions

- Add all ingredients to the bread machine in the suggested order by the manufacturer.
- Select quick bread cycle—press start.
- Enjoy fresh bread.

6.6 Keto Focaccia

(Prep time: 10 minutes | Total time: 3 hours 10 minutes)

Ingredients

- 3 cups of whole wheat flour
- 1 cup of lukewarm water
- 2 teaspoons of chopped garlic
- 1 and a half teaspoons of active dry yeast
- 2 tablespoons of olive oil
- 1 tablespoon of chopped fresh rosemary
- half teaspoon of salt
- 1 and a half teaspoons of chopped fresh rosemary
- 1 tsp. of xanthan gum

Instructions

- Add all ingredients to the bread machine in the suggested order by the manufacturer.
- Select dough cycle. Press start.
- Take the dough out from the bread machine and put in a 12" pizza pan. With clean fingers, dimple the bread.

- Brush with olive oil and sprinkle fresh rosemary. Cover with wrap.
- Let the oven preheat to 400 F.
- Bake for 20-25 minutes, until golden brown.
- Serve fresh bread.

6.7 Oregano Onion Focaccia

(Prep time: 10 minutes | Total time: 3 hours 40 minutes)

Ingredients

Dough

- 3/4 cup of water
- 1 tablespoon of sugar
- 2 tablespoons of olive oil
- 1 and a half teaspoons of yeast
- 1 teaspoon of salt
- 2 tablespoons of shredded parmesan cheese
- 3/4 cup of shredded mozzarella cheese
- 2 cups of almond flour
- 3/4 tsp. of xanthan gum

Toppings

- 2 minced garlic cloves
- 3 tablespoons of butter
- 2 medium sliced onions

Instructions

- Add all ingredients of dough to the bread machine in the suggested order by the manufacturer.
- Select dough cycle. Press start.

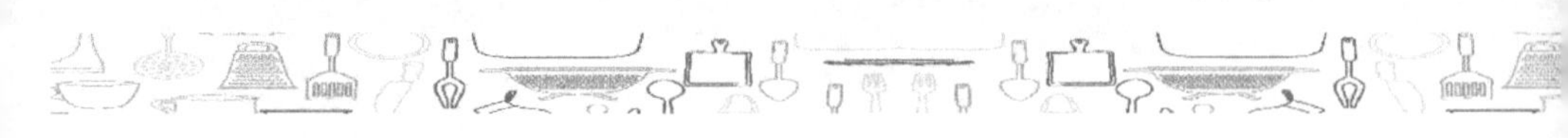

- Meanwhile, melt butter on medium flame and sauté garlic and onion until caramelized.
- Take the dough out on an oiled baking sheet. Make the dough into 12" circles. Let it rise for half an hour until it doubles.
- Let the oven preheat to 400 F. with a wooden spoon, make a depression into the dough.
- Place topping on the dough. Bake for 15-20 minutes until golden brown.   Enjoy fresh bread.

6.8 Keto Baguette

(Prep time: 10 minutes | Total time: 2 hours 40 minutes)

Ingredients

- 1 and 1/4 cups of warm water
- 1 teaspoon of salt
- 3 and a half cups of gluten-free flour
- One and a half tsp of xanthan gum
- 1 package of active dry yeast

Instructions

- Add all ingredients to the bread machine in the suggested order by the manufacturer.
- Select dough cycle. Press start.
- Take the dough out on a clean, floured surface.
- Cut into half pieces. Make a 12" long shape from each piece.
- Put on an oiled baking pan. Cover with a warm towel.
- Let it rise for one hour. Let the oven preheat to 450 F.
- Bake for 15-20 minutes, until golden brown.
- Serve fresh.

Chapter 7: Gluten-Free Breads

7.1 Gluten-Free Peasant Bread

(Prep time: 10 minutes | Total time: 3 hours 40 minutes)

Ingredients

- 1 and a half tablespoons of vegetable oil
- 2 teaspoons of xanthan gum
- 1 and a half cups of warm water
- 1 teaspoon of cider vinegar

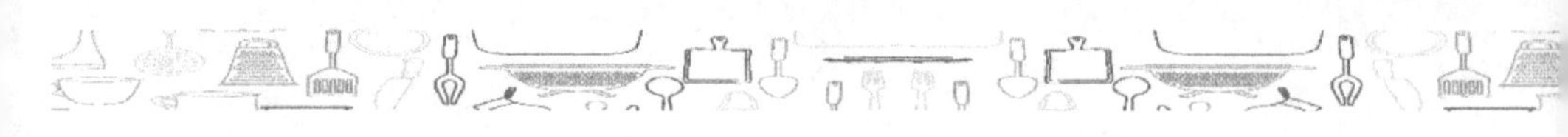

- 2 and a half cups of gluten-free baking flour
- 1 tablespoon of active dry yeast
- 1 teaspoon of salt
- 2 whole eggs
- 1 tablespoon of white sugar

Instructions

- Place all ingredients into the bread machine in the suggested order by the manufacturer.
- Select basic cycle. Light crust. Press start.
- Enjoy fresh bread.

7.2 Gluten-Free Hawaiian Loaf

(Prep time: 10 minutes | Total time: 3 hours 40 minutes)

Ingredients

- 3 tablespoons of oil
- 3 and a half tablespoons of honey
- 2 whole eggs
- 1 cup of pineapple juice (room temperature)
- 4 cups of gluten-free Flour
- 3 tablespoons of skim dry milk
- 1 tablespoon of fast-rising yeast

Instructions

- Add all ingredients to the bread machine in the suggested order by the manufacturer.
- Select the gluten free cycle. Dark crust. Press start.
- Enjoy fresh bread.

7.3 Vegan Gluten-Free Bread

(Prep time: 10 minutes | Total time: 1 hour 45 minutes)

Ingredients

- 1 and a half tsp of xanthan gum
- Olive oil: 2 tbsp.
- Gluten-free flour blend: 2.2 cups
- 1 tbsp. of ground flax seeds
- Warm water: 1.6 cups
- 2 and 1/4 tsp of Easy Bake yeast
- 1 tsp of sea salt

Instructions

- Add all ingredients to the bread machine in the suggested order by the manufacturer.
- Select a gluten-free cycle—press start.
- Before the baking cycle begins, brush olive oil on the loaf and sprinkle seeds.
- Enjoy fresh bread.

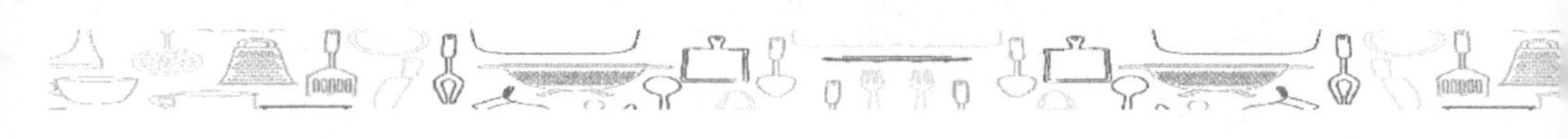

7.4 Greek Easter Bread

(Prep time: 10 minutes | Total time: 2 hours 40 minutes)

Ingredients

- Half cup of caster sugar
- 3 whole eggs, lightly whisked
- 2 tsp. Of dried yeast
- 4 and a half cups of baker's flour
- 2 teaspoons of Mahlepi
- Half cup + 1 tbsp. of butter melted
- 1/3 cup of milk
- 1/3 cup of lukewarm water
- Juice from half of an orange, grated rinds

Instructions

- Add 1 tbsp. of sugar, water, and yeast to the machine's pan. Mix lightly and let it rest for 8 minutes.
- Add the rest of the ingredients to the pan also. Select dough cycle and press start.
- Preheat the oven to 338 F. prepare a baking tray by spraying cooking oil and placing parchment paper.

- Take the dough out and cut it into three pieces. Roll the pieces into sausages shapes and pinch at one end.
- Braid the dough. Pinch the top and bottom and make a circle.
- Take three eggs and color them differently. Fit the eggs into the circled dough and let it rest for 20 minutes.
- Bake in the oven for 20 minutes after glazing with egg wash until.
- Serve.

7.5 Fiji Sweet Potato Bread

(Prep time: 10 minutes | Total time: 2 hours 15 minutes)

Ingredients

- 2 teaspoons of active dry yeast
- 1 cup of mashed sweet potatoes (plain)
- 4 cups of bread flour
- 1 and a half teaspoons of salt
- Water: 2 tablespoons + half cup
- 2 tablespoons of softened butter
- 1/3 cup of dark brown sugar
- chopped pecans
- 1 teaspoon of vanilla extract
- 2 tablespoons of dry milk powder
- 1/4 teaspoon (each) of ground nutmeg & cinnamon

Instructions

- Add all ingredients, except pecans, to the bread machine in the suggested order by the manufacturer.
- Select white bread cycle—light crust and Press start.
- Add nuts at the ingredient signal.
- Enjoy fresh bread.

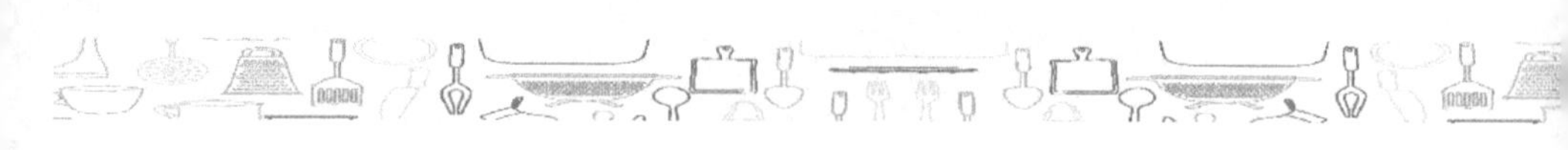

7.6 Za'atar Bread

(Prep time: 10 minutes | Total time: 3 hours 40 minutes

Ingredients

- 3 and a half cups of bread flour
- 1 and 1/3 cups of water
- 1 and 1/4 teaspoons of sugar
- 2 and a half tablespoons of olive oil
- 2 tsp. of quick yeast
- 1 teaspoon of salt
- 2 and a half teaspoons of Za'atar

Instructions

- Add all ingredients to the bread machine in the suggested order by the manufacturer.
- Select quick bread cycle—medium crust and Press start.

7.7 Pizza Dough

(Prep time: 10 minutes | Total time: 1 hour 40 minutes)

Ingredients

- 1 and a half tablespoons of vegetable oil
- 1 and a half teaspoons of salt
- 1 and a half teaspoons of active dry yeast
- 3 and 3/4 cups of bread flour
- 1 and a half cups of water
- 1 tablespoon + 1 teaspoon of sugar

Instructions

- Add all ingredients to the bread machine in the suggested order by the manufacturer.
- Select dough cycle. Press start.
- Let the oven preheat to 400 F.
- Take the dough out and roll it into one inch thick.
- Drizzle oil and let it rest for 10-15 minutes.
- Add pizza sauce and toppings of your choice.
- Bake for 20-25 minutes.
- Enjoy the fresh pizza.

7.8 Milk & Honey Bread

(Prep time: 10 minutes | Total time: 2 hours 10 minutes)

Ingredients

- 3 cups of bread flour
- Milk: 1 cup + 1 tbsp.
- 3 tablespoons of melted butter
- 2 teaspoons of active dry yeast
- 1 and a half teaspoons of salt
- 3 tablespoons of honey

Instructions

- Add all ingredients to the bread machine in the suggested order by the manufacturer.
- Select basic cycle. Medium crust and Press start.
- Enjoy fresh bread.

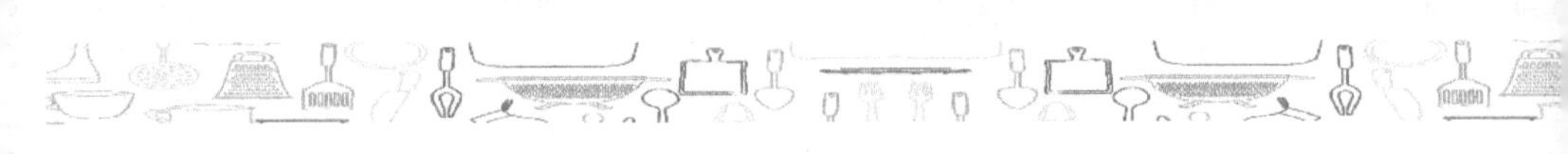

Chapter 8: Oven Recipes to Bread Machine Conversion

The bread machine can label a 1-pound, 1.5 pounds, or 2-pound loaf. What it means is the "flour capacity." Review the manufacturer's booklet of the bread machine to calculate any individual bread machine's flour capability. You can check if the manufacturer's booklet calls for 3-4 cups of flour regularly, then it is your bread machine's capacity. Now you can convert oven recipes to bread machine recipes.

These are general flour capacities that yield a certain pound of bread loaf:

- The bread machine that yields 1-pound uses 2 or 2-3/4 cups of flour
- Bread machine that yields 1.5 pound uses 3-4 cups of flour
- Bread machine that yields 2-pound use 4 to 5 and a half cups of flour

Here are some measurements to help you convert the oven to bread machine recipes:

- Reduce the amount of yeast to 1 tsp for a 1.5-pound bread machine and 1 and 1/4 tsp. for a two-pound machine.

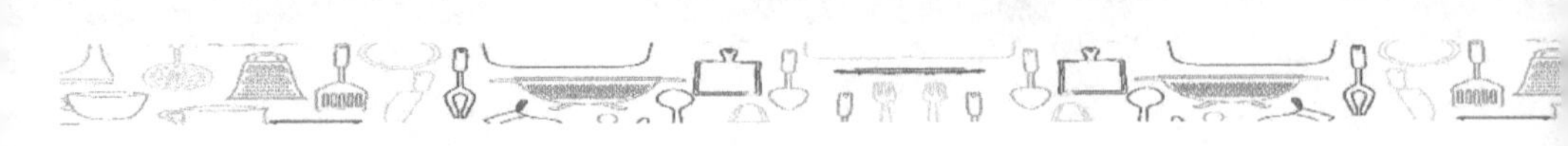

- Reduce the flour to three cups for a 1.5-pound bread machine and 4 cups for a 2-pound bread machine.
- Reduce the other ingredients as well, along with flour and yeast.
- If a recipe calls for 2 or different kinds of flour, add the flour quantities and use it to decrease the formula. The total amount of flour used can be either 3 -4 cups based on the bread's size.
- Use 1-3 tbsp. of gluten flour in a bread machine with all-purpose flour, or only use bread flour, which is a better option. If you are using any rye flour, must combine with 1 tbsp. of gluten flour if even the base is bread flour.
- All ingredients should be at room temperature and added to the bread machine in the manufacturer's suggested order.
- Add any nuts, raisins, dried fruits to the ingredient signal, or as the manufacturer's booklet specifies.
- If you are using only dough cycle, try to handle the dough with a little more flour after taking out from the machine, so it will be easy to handle.

- Use the whole-grain cycle if the bread machine has one, for whole-wheat, rye, and any grain flour.
- Always try to keep the recipe or any additional changes made to the recipe safe for future references.
- Use the sweet bread cycle with a light crust for rich and sweet bread.

8.1 Conversion Tables

Here are some conversion tables to help you measure recipes accurately.

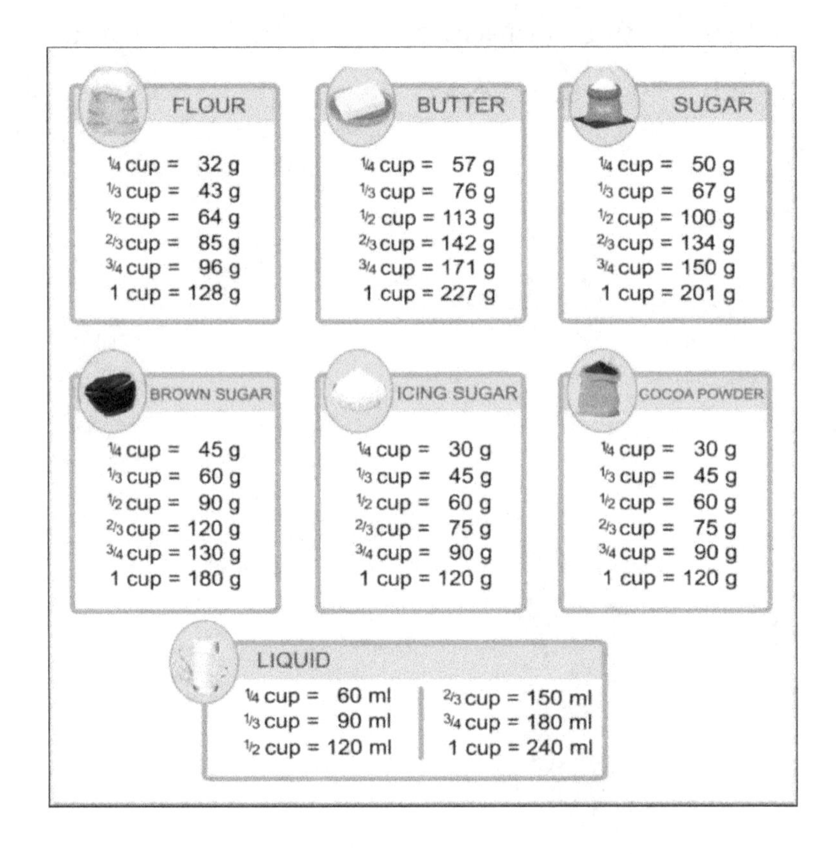

FLOUR	BUTTER	SUGAR
¼ cup = 32 g	¼ cup = 57 g	¼ cup = 50 g
⅓ cup = 43 g	⅓ cup = 76 g	⅓ cup = 67 g
½ cup = 64 g	½ cup = 113 g	½ cup = 100 g
⅔ cup = 85 g	⅔ cup = 142 g	⅔ cup = 134 g
¾ cup = 96 g	¾ cup = 171 g	¾ cup = 150 g
1 cup = 128 g	1 cup = 227 g	1 cup = 201 g

BROWN SUGAR	ICING SUGAR	COCOA POWDER
¼ cup = 45 g	¼ cup = 30 g	¼ cup = 30 g
⅓ cup = 60 g	⅓ cup = 45 g	⅓ cup = 45 g
½ cup = 90 g	½ cup = 60 g	½ cup = 60 g
⅔ cup = 120 g	⅔ cup = 75 g	⅔ cup = 75 g
¾ cup = 130 g	¾ cup = 90 g	¾ cup = 90 g
1 cup = 180 g	1 cup = 120 g	1 cup = 120 g

LIQUID	
¼ cup = 60 ml	⅔ cup = 150 ml
⅓ cup = 90 ml	¾ cup = 180 ml
½ cup = 120 ml	1 cup = 240 ml

CUPS	TBSP	TSP	ML
1	16	48	250
3/4	12	36	175
2/3	11	32	150
1/2	8	24	125
1/3	5	16	70
1/4	4	12	60
1/8	2	6	30
1/16	1	3	15

If you want to double the recipes:

Original Recipe	Double Recipe
1/8 tsp	**1/4 tsp**
1/4 tsp	**1/2 tsp**
1/2 tsp	**1 tsp**
3/4 tsp	**1 1/2 tsp**
1 tsp	**2 tsp**
1 Tbsp	**2 Tbsp**
2 Tbsp	**4 Tbsp or 1/4**
1/8 cup	**1/4 cup**
1/4 cup	**1/2 cup**
1/3 cup	**2/3 cup**
1/2 cup	**1 cup**
2/3 cup	**1 1/3 cups**
3/4 cup	**1 1/2 cups**
1 cup	**2 cups**
1 1/4 cup	**2 1/2 cups**
1 1/3 cup	**2 2/3 cups**
1 1/2 cup	**3 cups**
1 2/3 cup	**3 1/3 cups**
1 3/4 cup	**3 1/2 cups**

Conclusion

Everybody is occupied in this busy day and age, but no one has time to bake bread from scratch, but with a bread machine, you only have to add precisely measured ingredients, and it will bake you fresh bread. The bread machine is easy to use. If one doesn't have the time to practice and have little training, but you also want fresh bread, this really is the machine for you. The bread machine can easily turn you into a baker. You will save money, time, be in charge of the food (the food that goes into your body), and eat fresh food. The bread maker does all the labor of kneading the dough and avoids the trial and error involved with the dough's readiness. To combine and knead the bread dough, one can use a stand mixer or a food processor. But you are offered the choice of completing the baking by the bread maker. So, it's a handy appliance that saves time.

Making the bread allows you to control over the products, as opposed to buying prepared bread. The bread machines are enjoyed by many, solely for the diet element. You get to select the ingredients, monitor or use substitutes for starch, milk, and other components with a bread machine. You will ensure the family a no-preservative product with a bread machine. Many people enjoy their machines for bread and jams and will not be without one. As gluten-free bread is often best when baked in the machine, many gluten-free diets consider this an indispensable appliance. For some, it appears like the excitement of baking fresh bread from scratch wears off easily. The entire thing is rendered so much simpler by the bread machine. Place the ingredients into the bread maker, push start, select the cycle you want, and that's all one has to do. The kitchen remains tidy, and waiting for the fresh bread to be ready is all that's you have left to do.

The schedule becomes critical if you bake bread regularly and despite the rigorous routine that most of us maintain and know so well. There are many benefits of using a bread machine. Most bread machines would have built-in times to avoid mixing, enable to rise, punch down the dough, and so on. Bread Machines will bake bread as well, clearly, but mixers can't. With its many benefits, jams, jellies, and sauces may also be made.

Bread machines are very useful. For all the reasons, I would certainly suggest it. The pros outweigh the cons, and you can enjoy delicious freshly baked bread with many flavors any time you want.

Recipe Index

CPSIA information can be obtained
at www.ICGtesting.com
Printed in the USA
BVHW010936170521
607539BV00011B/258